The changing geography of economic activity

G000113777

A level

Geography Studies

Stephen Roulston

For Marie, Fergus, Patrick and Caitlin.

© Stephen Roulston
2001

Stephen Roulston (BEd, MA, DPhil) taught Geography briefly at Foyle and Londonderry College, and then moved to Ballymena Academy becoming Head of the Geography Department. Following three years' secondment as a Geography Field Officer with NEELB, he became a NINE/C2K Consultant in 2001.

Photographs on pages 6, 10 & 24
© Stephen Roulston

Designed by Colourpoint Books.
Printed by Nicholson & Bass Ltd.

Cover: *Police guard the premises of Nike during a World Trade Organisation meeting in Seattle, USA, in November 1999 (see page 31). Popperfoto/Reuters*

ISBN 1 898392 90 0

Colourpoint Books

Unit D5, Ards Business Centre
Jubilee Road
NEWTOWNARDS
County Down
Northern Ireland
BT23 4YH
Tel: 028 9182 0505
Fax: 028 9182 1900
E-mail: info@colourpoint.co.uk
Web-site: www.colourpoint.co.uk

Introduction

Primary, secondary and tertiary economic activities have changed and continue to change. In this booklet we will examine the causes and effects of some of these changes and a number of brief case studies will be outlined. Finally we will look at how the different types of economic activity are increasingly being integrated as, inexorably, the world moves towards a global economy.

That there are changes in these economic activities is clear from **Resource 1**. Since the first census in 1841 we can see a decline in those involved in primary industry in the UK. Secondary industry dominated then and, apart from a brief dip in 1931, remained the most important industry in the UK until the 1960s when overtaken by tertiary industry. Tertiary industry still dominates but, with vertical integration and globalisation, the divisions between the sectors of industry are becoming increasingly blurred. Many large companies are now involved in all sectors of the economy: from producing the raw materials, processing them and often packaging, transporting and even marketing them.

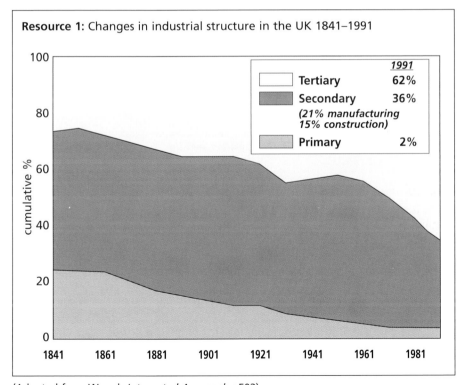

Resource 1: Changes in industrial structure in the UK 1841–1991

Legend (1991):
- Tertiary — 62%
- Secondary — 36% (21% manufacturing 15% construction)
- Primary — 2%

(Adapted from Waugh *Integrated Approach* p502)

3

Chapter 1

Agriculture

Agriculture has been practiced for over 10,000 years and, during most of that time, the farming systems developed in harmony with the local environment. Technological advances always influenced agricultural practices as breeds and seeds have been improved and as tools for working the land were made more sophisticated. However it is only recently that technology has allowed widespread specialisation and intensification. This has had positive effects in terms of food production but has had some negative consequences as well. Agriculture has moved from something that worked within an environment to a system that, in many places, attempts to work independently of the local environment. From relying on local inputs (of seeds, labour and fertiliser for example), agriculture increasingly uses inputs which are not found in the local environment. Markets too are changing and agriculture is now very much a part of the global economy.

While agriculture has continually evolved and adapted to technological change, a number of periods of rapid change have been identified which have been termed 'agricultural revolutions'. The first of these was when crops and livestock were first domesticated 10,000 years ago; the second began in England between the late sixteenth and mid-eighteenth centuries. It was marked by new farming practices such as crop rotation and the development of technologies which produced more food more effectively for rising urban populations.

In the last 50 years, a third revolution has taken place, this time started in the USA. This agricultural revolution again resulted in an increase in agricultural production and was based on further mechanisation, chemical inputs and food processing. As with earlier revolutions it too produced declining labour requirements with associated social effects in the countryside. There have also been considerable economic, political and environmental effects from these changes. For example, in 1985, the European Union spent 70% of its annual budget on the Common Agricultural Policy (CAP), much of it given as subsidies to farmers to encourage an increase in production. Other countries were restricted by tariffs on agricultural imports imposed by the EU to make foreign foodstuffs more expensive. A range of environmental effects has also been laid at the door of this 'industrialisation' of agriculture – from nitrate pollution of the groundwater to the destruction of hedgerows and wetlands.

The gathering speed of further agricultural change in the 1990s has heralded what some are calling another revolution. It is associated with biotechnology, the globalisation of agriculture and a move towards international free trade. While it is too early to predict the full social, environmental, political and economic impact of these changes, they are already starting to be felt.

Changes to agriculture

As farms have become increasingly mechanised larger fields are required, created by the removal of field boundaries. These large fields can then be planted with the same crop – a considerable saving to the farmer because of increased economies of scale. Large machines such as combine harvesters require large fields if they are to work efficiently and the removal of hedges also increases the amount of land available to the farmer. However their removal results in a less attractive landscape and a loss of wildlife. Estimates vary widely, but in the UK up to 130,000 km of hedgerows were removed between 1984 and 1990, nearly a quarter of the total. Those plants and animals which thrived in hedgerows, because of their similarity to woodland fringes, cannot survive in the monoculture that replaces the network of small fields.

Large farms benefit from buying inputs in bulk, reducing their costs. They can also be more efficient in the use of labour and power. Since they produce outputs in large quantities, this too can enhance their prospects of securing a good price for their product. Many of these large units developed by amalgamation with smaller neighbouring farms to increase the size of the original holding. The UK has the largest farm units in the EU but, within the UK, there are great differences in farm size, as indicated in **Resource 2**. The high proportion of large farms in Scotland may be a consequence of large hill tracts given over to estates, often run for absentee landlords. Many of the very large agricultural units in England may be large cereal farms. In Lincolnshire in the 1999 agricultural census, for example, there were 575 holdings with more than 100 hectares of wheat. Northern Ireland has relatively few very large farms. This may be a consequence of climate or of topography, but may also indicate that farm amalgamations have not yet had the impact that they have had in England.

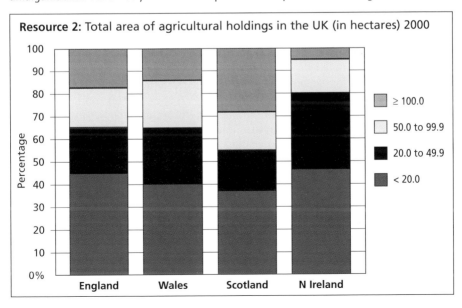

Resource 2: Total area of agricultural holdings in the UK (in hectares) 2000

Resource 3: Abandoned farmhouse in an upland area of Northern Ireland

As neighbouring farms amalgamate this is both a reflection of, and a cause of, reduced rural population levels, at least in remoter areas (See **Resource 3**). In Northern Ireland there were 2000 farms fewer in 2001 than in 1997. Some of this reduction may be farms in marginal land which were abandoned and some due to changes in use, to urban or to forestry for example, but much was likely to have been the result of the continuing process of farm amalgamation.

Agriculture has also undergone a transformation in its use of technologically advanced farming processes. Precision farming is an infant technology which is being developed, largely in the USA, and has the potential to revolutionise farming. There are two approaches:

- mapping soil characteristics using a Global Positioning System (GPS) and using this digital map to vary the application of chemicals to the soil automatically, again using GPS and computer sensor technology. If just one patch of a field is shown to need nitrogen-based fertiliser, for example, only in that patch will it be applied and at the precise levels required;
- using real-time sensors to provide information about soil and crops with immediate impact on rates of application of chemicals by sprayers and so on.

Proponents of precision farming point to the savings that can be made by the farmer by only applying pesticides, for example, to those parts of fields that require them, and the consequent minimisation of environmental damage. The next technology is said to be auto-steering, removing the need for a full-time human operator. This will facilitate night-time spraying and reduce labour costs. However the costs involved would be beyond the means of smaller farmers. Indeed only large companies sub-contracted to spray large farms are able to make full use of this technology at present – it is estimated that the break-even size for using the complete precision farming technology is over 6,000 hectares.

Inputs are also changing. Genetically modified (GM) crops are being produced which have a gene from a different species introduced into them. This may make them resistant to pests or to weedkillers (so that crops can be sprayed but only weeds will be killed), able to be stored for longer in good condition, have a shortened growing time and so on. Biotechnology companies claim that these will increase harvests and protect the environment but many conservationists are concerned that GM crops may damage the environment. They fear that the altered gene may be transferred to wild species of plants, creating 'superweeds'. Additionally, despite official assurances to the contrary, some people believe that GM foods may not be safe for human consumption.

Those changes that have happened to farming in More Economically Developed Countries (MEDCs), and those that are just beginning, have increased agricultural output. For example, milk yields in the Netherlands increased by almost 15% between 1980 and 1990. Intensive farming of poultry has lowered the costs of producing eggs and poultry meat. Farming is often termed **agribusiness** – which can reduce costs still further by linking with processing or marketing operations.

Consequences of changes in agriculture

While modern farming may be more productive than ever, this has often had a negative impact on the natural environment. Fertiliser use has grown with increases in both nitrogen based artificial fertiliser and phosphate-rich slurry from fodder fed animals. When applied to the fields, this can leach into groundwater and streams and rivers. The increase in nutrients can cause eutrophication and a loss of species diversity, especially in ponds and ditches, which in turn damages the wider ecosystem. Biodiversity has decreased as intensive farming has increased. For example, in Britain, species-rich wetlands have been ploughed and sown with rye grass seed. This is harvested for silage production. While more efficient for meat production than the traditional grazing patterns and haymaking techniques of the 1940s and before, the modern farming regime operates at the cost of the diverse plant life and the associated insects and other elements of the ecosystem. As Alison Rae has said "the land still looks green, but it no longer supports the same specialised wetland wildlife".

People too have faced changes in the countryside. This is particularly true in hill farming areas. Falling incomes in Less Favoured Areas (LFAs) have threatened the future of farming in these areas. The average income of Welsh LFA farmers was as low as £3,600 in 1999 for example. Limited prospects for future earnings and uncertain incomes persuade many young people not to consider farming as a career. In Northern Ireland there were 29,890 farms in 2000, which provided work for 60,339 people. However only 65% of these farms are able to support one person or more working full-time. As the numbers of farm workers has decreased, and the remaining farm workforce ages, and rural incomes from farming decline, inevitably rural communities and the services on which they rely such as shops and schools become increasingly threatened. This can cause a migration out of remote rural areas, although those rural areas accessible to commuters may experience counterurbanisation. The move towards bigger and even more highly mechanised farms in the more favoured areas of Britain, managed perhaps by an employee of a large conglomeration, seems set to continue. The future for smaller units such as hill farms is much less clear.

There has been some movement by consumers towards organic produce, although it makes up less than 5% of UK production at present. Many of the large agribusiness corporations are beginning to get interested in organic food as a niche market. For example, in the UK, Unilever, a strong proponent of GM crops, have bought Go Organic. In the USA organic farming is now worth $7.7 billion and is dominated by agribusiness interests. These include Horizon, which has been described as the Microsoft of organic milk, controlling 70% of this specialist retail market. However, much of this milk is produced in 'factory farms' with thousands of cows confined to a small fenced area being fed organic grain but with no grazing available. The milk is then 'ultrapasturised', a high-heat process that allegedly destroys the enzymes and many of the vitamins in the milk, but allows it to be transported long distances. Thus organic farming, if it becomes a mainstream farming practice, may be drawn towards monoculture and factory-type farming, the very antithesis of what many people consider as 'organic' farming.

The appointment, in August 2001, of Lord Haskins to spearhead agricultural recovery after the foot and mouth outbreak in the UK signals changes ahead for UK farming. He predicts that the number of farms in Britain will halve in the next 20 years. He said: "farms will get bigger and that's a good thing." Those who believe that such a change might not be such a good thing point to the fact that Lord Haskins is Chairman of Northern Foods, a food-processing conglomerate. As for organic production, he has said: "... that's for the birds. Agriculture has got to strive to be more competitive and more productive."

Case study: Changes in agriculture in Brittany, France

Breton agriculture was already undergoing dramatic transformation in 1975, when Phlipponneau wrote about it, and Dalton and Canevet have charted these changes to the present day. Brittany was a relatively remote and economically marginal area until comparatively recently. It is now one of the most important agricultural regions in France, with double the average regional agricultural output – a transformation that has taken only 50 years. In 1950 Brittany had 6.1% of France's agricultural land and produced 6.6% of the country's agricultural output. In 1995 it was producing 13.6%.

Breton farmers currently produce over half of all the pig meat and duck meat in France, 47% of all the eggs, 32% of all the veal and 23% of French milk. The advancement of Breton agriculture has helped to make France the leading producer (by value) of foodstuffs in Europe.

Brittany had long been famous for its production of fresh vegetables but its agricultural economy is now dominated by arable cropping, mostly of maize and cereals, as fodder for livestock and the production of dairy products, beef, poultry and pigmeat.

The major impetus to change from the traditional agriculture of the region has been the financial incentives of the Common Agriculture Policy. Brittany had been dominated by tiny farms with very small grassy fields, often planted with apple trees, separated by high banks with strips of woodland from which firewood and building materials were harvested. This agricultural landscape is called **bocage**. Many of these farms were rented and, with insecure tenancies, there was little incentive for farmers to improve their farms. With limited individual economic power, farm inputs were relatively expensive for the small farmer and marketing produce effectively was also difficult. There was much emigration from the region leaving an ageing agricultural population. Funds from the CAP allowed the agricultural economy to be transformed. Older farmers were given incentives to retire and the released land was used in farm amalgamation and consolidation. Larger blocks of land replaced the small fragmented farms, a process is known as **remembrement parcellaire**, and security of tenure was provided. Cooperatives, which could get better rates for farm inputs and market farm produce more effectively than individual farms, were formed. New technical advances and scientific approaches to farming processes were encouraged also. Together these developments changed Breton agriculture, and the wider Breton countryside, in a very short time.

While Brittany lost some of its agricultural land to urbanisation, and marginal land has been abandoned, agricultural production has increased as a result of more intensive use being made of the remaining farmland. The small fields with natural grazing which often gave a low yield were replaced by large fields with crops of grass sown for silage. Maize and cereal crops are also widely grown as fodder crops for the livestock of the region.

The numbers of dairy cattle in Brittany grew from about 1 million in 1950 to a peak of 1.6 million in 1980. At the same time the average milk yield grew from 1300 litres per cow per year to almost 4000 litres. After the 1980s, milk quotas (limits to milk production applied to individual farmers) were imposed by the EU to reduce overproduction of milk and this has led to a drop in the numbers of dairy cattle. Now back close to the 1950 number, overall milk production has only fallen by 10% as milk yields per animal have continued to rise (now at 5600 litres per cow per year).

Both the poultry meat and pigmeat sectors have had enormous growth. These are increasingly being intensively farmed in large factory style units. While an average pig unit, for example, in the 1950s would have contained an average of 12 sows, in the 1990s this figure reached 90. Phlipponneau reports pig units with up to 10,000 animals being set up as early as the mid-1970s in the eastern Côtes-du-Nord and Finistère departments. Both pigmeat and poultry production are strongly integrated with the

Resource 4: Modern Breton farm, 2001

agrifood industry for processing and marketing.

Agrifood industries have been a major factor in modernising Breton farming and they provide 31% of all industrial employment in Brittany. Poultry and pigmeat agrifood industries tend to be set up by investment from outside the region by national or multinational companies and provide much employment. For example, 10,000 people work in farms producing pigs. In 'upstream' industries 1850 are employed in providing foodstuffs for the pig units. 'Downstream' from the farms there are 4300 jobs in abattoirs and 5750 in processing the meat. There are a further 700 jobs in management and about 3000 in transport of the various inputs and outputs.

The changes to Breton agriculture have had effects on the rural landscape and the region's hydrology and people.

A lot of the **bocage** has been destroyed (a process the French call **debocagement**) in order to create larger fields, more effective for producing fodder crops. In many areas the average field size was tripled and some fields of over 15 hectares were created, this in a region where, despite **remembrement**, average farm size was less than 30 hectares. The reduction of biodiversity by the removal of the strips of woodland is every bit as great as that associated with hedgerow removal in East Anglia.

Debocagement has led to an increase in runoff, as the vegetation which previously stored some of the rainwater was removed. This has led to lowered levels of channel flow during periods of low rainfall and to local droughts. Since intensively farmed livestock require large amounts of water, there has been a need to construct small reservoirs around the region.

Brittany applies more fertiliser to its fields than anywhere else in France, largely as a result of the intensification of arable farming for fodder. This has led to an increase in nitrate levels in groundwater. Between 1960 and 1980 levels have been estimated to have increased by 5 times. In some areas of intensive livestock farming, slurry disposal is also a cause of water pollution. The high levels of pollution are thought to have been exacerbated by loss of bocage which otherwise would have absorbed some of the nitrates.

The number of farms in Brittany has declined from 235,000 in 1955 to less than 80,000 in 1994. Employment in agriculture has fallen from 21.1% in 1970 to 9.4% in 1994. Falling employment before 1970 affected farm labourers most and then family helpers. Most of the decline in recent years has been in the farmers themselves and farm populations have fallen from 900,000 in 1955 to 328,000 in 1992. Brittany had traditionally been an area of outmigration, especially to Paris. This is no longer the case. Young Bretons are likely to remain in the region although many move to coastal areas. As farms become more industrialised and farming communities continue to be fragmented, rural society continues to be under pressure.

These changes have not been welcomed by all. Jose Bové, a sheep farmer and now an international celebrity, has become a hero to those who are fighting against the changes to agricultural practices in France. He was arrested in 1998 for leading 200 farmers in the destruction of GM corn being field tested by a large Multinational Corporation and, in 2000, he led the protests against McDonald's restaurants in France. These have been targeted by his organisation, The Farmers Confederation, in demonstrations against globalisation. Bové was arrested in the 2000 demonstration for destroying the building site for a McDonald's restaurant in Southern France. The choice of McDonald's as Bové's target was symbolic of the perceived link between the fast-food giant and issues related to the loss of local control – a process that has been called 'McDonaldization' by George Ritzer. Bové said: "Either we accept intensive production and the huge reduction in the number of farmers in the sole interests of the World Market, or we create a farmer's agriculture for the benefit of everyone."

Chapter 2

Manufacturing Industry

Secondary or manufacturing industry is the transformation of raw materials into products. Inevitably these industries have an impact on the environment. A labour intensive process in the past, it is increasingly becoming mechanised. Improved methods of manufacture and specialised production methods, have led to increased efficiency. As productivity rises, the associated mechanisation has led to manufacturing industry employing a smaller proportion of the workforce. Some of the manufacturing workforce lost in MEDCs is relocated to LEDCs.

While a declining workforce is a relatively new phenomenon, manufacturing has always been a dynamic operation. Production on a small scale in people's homes or in small workshops (domestic industry) was superseded by factory production in the late 18th and 19th centuries in Britain. This led to increased output and stimulated further mechanisation. Textiles and engineering products began to be mass-produced – large-scale production of this kind was found to be efficient and outputs could be maximised. In 1908, Henry Ford opened the world's first large scale car assembly plant in Detroit. Cars were mass-produced using an assembly line with each worker having a closely defined role in the production of the vehicles – a process called **Fordism**. Car manufacture was to be the first of many industries applying those principles. The social consequences of such manufacturing were huge. Large factories required labour and thus factories stimulated the growth of settlements. Many cities such as Detroit became dependent for their economic prosperity upon the industries that led to their growth.

There has been much automation of the manufacturing process since Fordism's early years and computers and robot technology continue to push this process forward. The organisation of those people still needed in the production line has also changed. Fordism, with people very specialised within the manufacturing process, is now viewed as too inflexible for the nature of today's manufacturing. Following developments in Japanese factories, most modern factories are now organised around teams operating quality control and continuous improvement of the manufacturing processes. These flexible, **lean production** methods are seen as vital to produce a manufacturing industry that can adapt to the rapidly changing technology of production and to changes in patterns of consumption.

Changing manufacturing

The location of manufacturing industry is influenced by a combination of many factors.
1 Raw materials/fuel:
    In 19th Century Britain much of the industry was located on or near to sources of fuels or raw materials such as on coal or iron ore fields or close to ports (for imported

raw materials). This was due to the difficulty of transportation at that time. Many of today's industries rely on fewer raw materials and are more fuel-efficient, or use more easily transported fuels than coal – oil or electricity for example. In consequence modern industries are less influenced by this factor.

2 Market:
This is now a more important influence on the location of many industries than any other factor. It is particularly important if the industry makes products which gain weight on manufacture, such as brewing. Industries which need to be responsive to changing trends, such as clothing manufacturers, benefit from being close to the markets that they serve.

3 Transport:
While once very important in deciding which locations for an industry would be economically viable, these costs are now a minor part of most manufacturing as transport networks have increased in efficiency. This has allowed industries, previously tied to one location, to locate elsewhere, although transport nodes are still attractive locations.

4 Labour supply:
The importance of this factor varies from one industry to another. While one industry may need to locate where there is plentiful, cheap and low skilled labour (such as in some LEDCs), another may require a smaller, but more skilled workforce. As industries become more mechanised the demand for low skilled labour declines and the need for a more highly skilled workforce becomes more important. In Britain, for example, there are now just over 4 million jobs in manufacturing compared to 6.5 million in 1980. (In the same period manufacturing output almost doubled)

5 Government policies:
Many governments have policies which try to influence the location of industry. Grants and other incentives may be made available to companies in an attempt to encourage them to locate in a particular place.

6 Globalisation:
Global markets and global production systems operated by Multinational Corporations (MNCs) such as Nike, Nestlé or Mitsubishi mean that these companies often have more say over the opening and closing of industrial operations than national governments.

Many industries have changed their distribution as the influence of these factors has changed. For example, clothing factories, once the basis of much of the industry in the North West of Northern Ireland, have largely shifted to low wage economies in countries such as Bangladesh and Thailand.

Vernon's **product life cycle model** (1966) suggests that a manufacturing product goes through a number of changes over time. As the product is developed, investment in Research and Development tends to be high. The location of the industry at this time will be influenced by personal decisions and may be in the home town of the industrialist. The product is supplied to a relatively small urban market but, with rapid growth of production, the need for automation and standardisation of production is

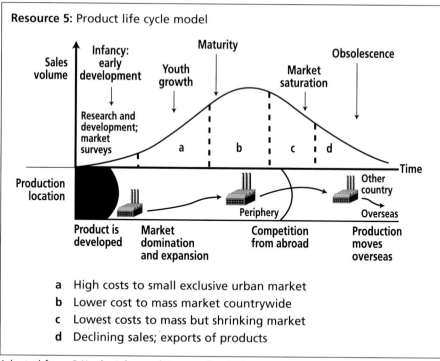

Resource 5: Product life cycle model

a   High costs to small exclusive urban market
b   Lower cost to mass market countrywide
c   Lowest costs to mass but shrinking market
d   Declining sales; exports of products

Adapted from G Nagle *Advanced Geography* p308

increased. The location of the industry may change at this time, moving to locations which maximise profits. As the product matures and the growth of domestic sales starts to level off and then to decline, it becomes important for the industry to seek new markets. At this stage it may become economic to move production abroad, closer to the newly opening markets there, exploiting opportunities for reducing labour costs.

The logic of this model is that *all* production will eventually move away from current industrial centres to be replaced with new products, for *their* early growth. It is a model which predicts globalisation, as manufacturing shifts from centres of innovation in the core to a low labour cost periphery. However the emergence of lean production methods in core areas may challenge the appropriateness of the product life cycle model in the future.

Many areas have specialised in the manufacture of one product, eg Detroit was the main car producing area in the USA. All specialised areas are vulnerable to changes in industrial location as the life cycle of those products matures. In many places the response to this vulnerability has been an attempt to diversify away from the traditional industry in order to widen the industrial base. Such **product diversification** leads to increased stability, particularly if the diversification is not into functionally linked enterprises.

Blackburn in Lancashire was dependent on cotton textiles for much of its employment and prosperity. In 1929 over 70% of those employed worked in cotton mills or in associated industries. By 1990 this had fallen to 9%, and the town had very high unemployment and associated social problems. The area still has relatively high unemployment (21%), but efforts have been made to reindustrialise the town and to diversify away from a dependence on textiles. Boosted by funds from a successful City Challenge Bid in the mid-1990s and from Single Regeneration Budget funding, the Borough of Blackburn with Darwen has had £115 million to invest over seven years. It is still more dependent on manufacturing than most other parts of the UK, with 37% of the total workforce in manufacturing, but its new industries, located in a number of Business and Technology Parks, include Whitbread brewery, Cable Components, Hi-Tec Plastics, Phillips Engineering and Chapman Envelopes. This diversification should make Blackburn's industrial structure more resilient to change than was the case when the area was dependent on textiles alone.

Consequences of changes in manufacturing

Deindustrialisation is the decline of secondary industries in an area as measured in falling output, either in real terms, or compared to other sectors of the economy. As a result fewer people are employed in manufacturing. Some sources distinguish between positive deindustrialisation, where the reductions in workforce are accompanied by rises in productivity and negative deindustrialisation, where productivity is also lost.

The causes of deindustrialisation are complex: some believe it to be an inevitable consequence of an economy coming to maturity. Others believe it is a result of complacency in some industries, with competitors able to steal an edge. Still others see deindustrialisation as the result of lack of investment in manufacturing. However none of these explanations is fully satisfactory and some geographers are now suggesting an explanation based on globalisation. As MNCs (see Chapter 4) become more powerful, they can more easily shift production, for example from high wage economies such as the UK to low wage economies such as Thailand. In this view deindustrialisation in MEDCs is caused by the actions of MNCs.

There are a number of consequences of deindustrialisation for MEDCs. Not all manufacturing will cease to operate in a deindustrialised area and pollution may continue from those plants which remain. Indeed, such will be the pressure for jobs in an area, it is likely that local opposition to pollution from an employer who remains would be muted. Industries are already allowed to pollute. For example, in the early 1990s, ICI was allowed to discharge 120 tonnes of sulphuric acid and 45 tonnes of cyanide into the seas around the UK each day. Many 'dirty industries' are being shifted from MEDCs to Less Economically Developed Countries (LEDCs) but, while pollution may decline, contaminated land will remain. In 2001 the long troubled steel mill in Sydney, Nova Scotia, Canada, closed down after more than a century of operation. The town's citizens remain affected by the residual contamination – an area known as the 'Tar Ponds' and thought to be the most polluted land in the world, but without the trade-off any more of the jobs that the mill had provided. The slow progress by the Canadian authorities to clean up the Tar Ponds has become a major political issue in the area.

Deindustrialisation will also produce a decline in industrial employment in MEDCs. Simultaneously there may be a growth in the service sector of the economy. In the UK in 2000, services made up two thirds of the economy with manufacturing making up only one fifth. These service jobs often require different skills than those developed by people employed in manufacturing. Of those people still working in manufacturing, technological advances in production techniques often require retraining for workers. Skills of communication and IT skills are much more important than before. In the new lean production factories of today, workers have to fit into teams and flexibility and adaptability will be valued. High technology and knowledge-based industries producing computer equipment, pharmaceuticals, biotechnology products and so on require particularly high skills and a well developed education infrastructure if they are to be successful.

Case study: Iron and Steel Industry in the UK

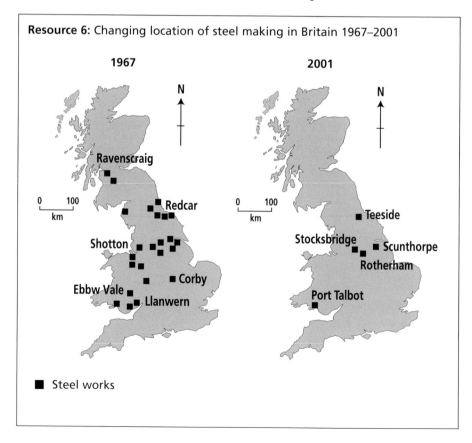

Resource 6: Changing location of steel making in Britain 1967–2001

1967

2001

Ravenscraig

Redcar

Shotton

Corby

Ebbw Vale

Llanwern

Teeside

Stocksbridge

Scunthorpe

Rotherham

Port Talbot

■ Steel works

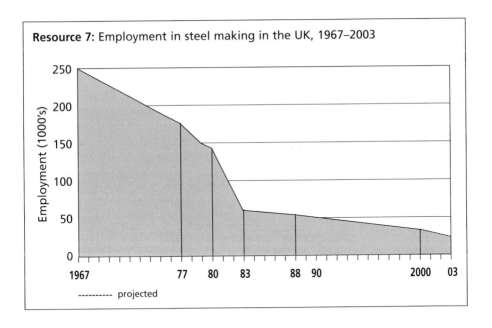

Resource 7: Employment in steel making in the UK, 1967–2003

Employment (1000's)

--------- projected

The geography of Iron and Steel production in the UK in 1967 was a consequence of many of the factors that affect the location of industries and their changing importance over time. Some steelworks were located on inland coalfields (eg Ebbw Vale), some close to iron ore deposits (eg Corby) and some on the coast (eg Shotton). These locations had evolved with time as raw materials became more or less available or important in the process of steel making. In 1967 the government took most of the iron and steel industry into public ownership (nationalisation), forming the British Steel Corporation (BSC). At that time BSC employed 250,000 workers in 24 large integrated iron and steelworks, and in a few smaller steelworks and ironworks and in iron ore terminals where ore was imported. In the decades following nationalisation, the Iron and Steel industry underwent very dramatic changes. The numbers of steelworks dropped dramatically, those remaining became larger and coastal locations became favoured. In 1994, the Conservative Government put the BSC back into private hands (privatisation) and the industry was further restructured and rationalised. In 1999 British Steel, as BSC had become, merged with a Dutch steel and aluminium manufacturer, Koninklijke Hoogovens, to form a new group: Corus. This group became reportedly the biggest steel maker in Europe and the third biggest in the world. By mid-2000, within a year of the merger, Corus was losing £20million each month.

Only four large steelworks remain: Port Talbot, Teeside, Scunthorpe and Rotherham/Stocksbridge. The other steelworks in Wales, in Llanwern, closed in the summer of 2001. The causes of these changes were a combination of falling demand, competition from other producers (especially from SE Asia) and denationalisation of the industry. The closures had an enormous impact on the number of workers employed in steelmaking in the UK. The 250,000 workers of 1967 became a mere 32,800 by 2000. Corus forecast that numbers will drop to 22,000 by 2003.

The closures and job losses had profound effects on the people who lived in the areas involved with steelmaking, particularly in those areas which depended on steel. For example the steelworks in Consett, in Derwentside, County Durham, with a population of just 36,000, had employed 5500 steelworkers in 1975. It finally closed in 1980 and, following the closure, many firms such as the local ball-bearing manufacturers closed soon after with even more job losses. The consequences for Consett were enormous. Unemployment rose to 28% in 1982 and this had a knock-on effect on services in Consett: many local pubs, shops and other businesses closed.

Derwentside Industrial Development Agency has done much to revitalise the area by attracting many small businesses, such as Derwent Valley Foods, makers of snack foods including the Phileas Fogg brand. From a situation in 1975 where the steelworks dominated employment, 70% of all industrial jobs are now in businesses of less than 25 people. However many of these new jobs do not require the skills of those made unemployed by the closure of the steelworks. Unemployment, especially among males, is still relatively high. In 1997 there was an 18.0% unemployment rate for males in Derwentside, compared to just 5.7% for females and 6.4% for Britain as a whole.

Even for those in areas close to the remaining steelworks, the chances of continuing employment are much reduced. Technological advances are largely responsible for increasing productivity but are also responsible for declining employment levels. For example, the Port Talbot steelworks in 1980 took 11.85 man-hours to produce 1 tonne of steel; by 1993 this had been reduced to just 2.85. The type of workforce needed has also changed. Increasingly, there are requirements for computer skills and Corus is now able to adopt a more pro-active equal opportunities programme to attract more women to jobs in steelworks.

Steelworks have always contributed to environmental problems such as air pollution. Friends of the Earth used the Government's own data for 1999 to calculate the value of its Air Quality Indicator, called by the government a 'key quality of life indicator'. This measures the average number of days on which air pollution levels for five main pollutants – ozone, particles, sulphur dioxide, nitrogen dioxide and carbon monoxide – exceeds safe limits. The study found that Port Talbot was the most polluted place in Wales and the second most polluted urban site in Britain, in terms of air quality. Air pollution levels in Port Talbot exceeded health standards on 82 days in 1999. The main cause was high levels of fine particles resulting from industrial activity and from road traffic. The data also showed the Port Talbot steel works were the second largest emitter of harmful dioxins in Britain. This was despite the investment in fume emission control equipment by British Steel at all its integrated sites by 1997.

Even when production of steel ceases there remain problems of pollution within the production sites themselves. Ravenscraig, closed by British Steel in 1992, posed major environmental problems. The cleanup at the 455 hectare site was the biggest industrial decontamination project in Britain and was expected to cost £25 million. After 30 years of steel making at Ravenscraig, the main problems were oils and some phytotoxic metals which stop plants growing. In total 1.8 million tonnes of contaminated materials were treated. All of this had to be completed before a start could be made on regeneration of the area in 1999.

This regeneration 'Masterplan' is expected to involve up to £500m of investment until about 2015 and is set to bring major benefits to both the Scottish and Lanarkshire economies. It will include up to 3400 houses, a technology park, a single-user industrial site of up to 92,900 square metres, retail space of 46,450 square metres, and leisure facilities. A spokesman for the Lanarkshire Development Agency said: "Since the launch of the Masterplan, the partners involved have made major progress in developing the project in terms of both planning and informing the local community".

Chapter 3

Tourism

Tourism is defined as visiting another region for a period of at least 24 hours. If domestic tourism, then the visit is within the country of origin, if international, a national boundary is crossed. The main reason for tourism is holidays, but sporting visits, attendance at religious festivals, business links and visits to friends and relatives also count as tourism. It has been growing at 6% each year and was estimated to be the largest industry in the world, in terms of employment, in 2000. The World Tourism Organisation calculated the worldwide revenue from tourism in 1996 to have been £258 billion, increased by more than 50% in just 5 years. The UK alone earned £30 billion through tourism in 1998. There are now about 550 million tourists crossing international boundaries every year, a figure that had been expected to double by 2010. The destruction of the World Trade Centre in New York by hijacked airliners in September 2001, and the reduction in air travel that followed that event, may mean that such predictions will have to be revised.

Changing tourism

The roots of modern tourism lie in the 17th century when the Grand Tour became a fashionable activity for the very rich. This involved trips, mainly to mainland Europe for the British aristocracy, to visit places rich in classical art such as Florence, Athens and Naples. Tourist resorts in Britain developed in the 18th century. These included spa towns (eg Tunbridge Wells) and sea bathing centres (eg Brighton). This form of tourism was an elite activity; it was not until the 1850s that tourism began to develop in scale and in economic importance, as it became an activity available to the masses.

Part of the social evolution of the manufacturing economy of Britain and other industrial economies led to, by the 1850s, an increase in holidays for factory workers, with many getting a full weeks holiday in the summer. This was paralleled by the development of a railway infrastructure. The railways had originally been seen as a means of moving goods and the very rich but the Railway Act of 1844 in Britain required all railway companies to provide third class carriages.

Resorts grew up to serve the needs of the industrial workers from the major cities of Victorian Britain. Blackpool and Morecambe grew up to serve as resorts for Manchester and Liverpool, Newcastle and Portrush for Belfast and so on. For a century mass tourism was confined to the seaside resort in Britain, but the middle classes increasingly discovered foreign travel.

From the 1950s the seaside holiday in Britain began to decline and started to be replaced with mass international tourism. Spanish coastal resorts became accessible to northern Europe with the advent of cheap flights and British workers found that foreign holidays were within their price range.

Mass foreign tourism continues to be a very important part of tourism. In 1999 the major destination for British tourists continued to be the Spanish Balearic Islands such as Ibiza. However there is some evidence that mass foreign tourism is beginning to decline. Increasingly tourists are rejecting the 'holiday camp' form of tourism and demanding new experiences. Tourism is being merged with other activities. Wildlife holidays, such as safaris in Kenya, combine environmental interest with travel. In sport, the Soccer World Cup and the Olympics have become major elements of global tourism. City breaks to cultural capitals such as Rome or Prague are other examples; there is even an increasing market in conflict tourism to places such as Belfast and Jerusalem. Some of these activities are still forms of mass tourism but, with the recognition that tourism can have damaging effects on environments and cultures, non-mass forms of tourism are also developing.

The future for tourism is relatively clear. Its growth is all but inevitable and its effects, both benign and malignant, will be felt on more and more of the globe.

Just as products of secondary industries display stages in their evolution, tourist destinations too have a **product life cycle**. The discovery and emergence of a tourist area is analogous to the development of a product. At first a few intrepid travellers visit the newly discovered place; only later do numbers start to rise as it becomes fashionable for rich tourists to travel there. As investors and tour operators move in, and tourist numbers increase, the destination becomes more developed, more accessible and more affordable – but less fashionable for the elite. The resort eventually reaches saturation and, unless rejuvenated in some way, is likely to decline as its popularity diminishes. Tourists no longer flock to the resort and investors and tour operators will

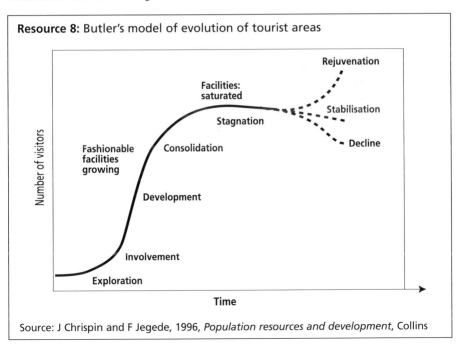

Resource 8: Butler's model of evolution of tourist areas

Source: J Chrispin and F Jegede, 1996, *Population resources and development*, Collins

move out to areas where profits will be greater. Thus new areas are developed as the product cycle begins in another area. A model of resort development has been produced by Dick Butler (**Resource 8**). Like most models, it simplifies reality and, while it helps us to understand the complex changes which may take place over time in such tourist destinations, it is possible to find resorts that have not followed the path suggested by the model.

The Product Cycle emphasises that tourism is an exploitative industry. When the tourism resources – scenery, isolation, scenic beauty, unspoilt natural features, welcoming local people and so on – have been 'consumed', and the area has lost much of its attraction, then the industry must discover new tourist areas to start the process of exploitation anew.

The view of tourism as a fashion industry has given rise to another interpretation of the process. The **pleasure periphery** emphasises the need by many tourists to seek out new destinations. In consequence the tourism wave spreads inexorably across the world. The limits of possible tourism in the 19th century were, for most people, confined to the local area; for Europeans this was Europe. By the 1940s Western Europeans had extended their pleasure periphery to the Eastern Mediterranean and Florida. This had extended by the 1970s to Tunisia and the Caribbean. In turn Kenya, Peru, and India

Resource 9: Dennis Tito (centre) the first tourist in space, with two Russian cosmonauts (Mikhail Metzel/AP)

became some of the 'places to go' for holidays in the 1980s. More remote areas, including Antarctica, became fashionable in the 1990s. In April 2001, Dennis Tito, a 60-year-old Californian millionaire, blasted off into space with two Russian cosmonauts. At a cost of £14 million for six days in the International Space Station, he became the first tourist in space and pushed further the pleasure periphery. As the tidal wave of fashion passes over some places and swamps others, few places are left to be 'discovered' or have escaped the influence of tourism.

Consequences of changes in tourism

The economy of an area can be positively affected by tourism. Employment in tourism may be seasonal, and often poorly paid, but it can generate a lot of income for local people. In areas where alternative means of employment are limited, it can act as an important stimulus to further economic investment and more employment. Where local people control the tourism, or have a significant share of the tourist facilities, the money brought in will largely stay within the local economy and will have spin off effects on other employment and on the local economy in general.

However tourism does not always bring those sorts of benefits to the economy of an area. In many cases the money, which *appears* to be brought into an area through tourism, is lost through **leakage**. This occurs when a proportion of the money brought into a place by tourists is lost to the area, reducing the economic benefit of the tourism. This can happen when tourists spend their money on products which have been manufactured outside the tourist destination. For example, a tourist in the Fermanagh Lakeland area may buy a souvenir which has been manufactured in France. Thus much of the value of the product will leak away from Fermanagh. Similarly the tourist can use services which are not locally owned. A high proportion of potential economic benefit for Fermanagh will leak away if the tourist stays in a hotel chain owned by a Multinational Corporation rather than a locally owned hotel, since much of the profits from the hotel chain will be directed back to the Multinational Corporation. If foreign workers are used in tourism, they may send much of their earnings home, increasing leakage. In Kenya it is estimated that 17% of tourist earnings leaks away from the Kenyan economy.

Places which attract a lot of tourists are called **honeypots**. For example, on the north coast of County Antrim, honeypots include the Giant's Causeway and Carrick-a-Rede Rope Bridge. Honeypots are also 'sticky' in that they tend to hold on to the tourists they attract. Neighbouring areas may be little affected by the tourists brought to a honeypot. Honeypots can suffer if they attract so many people that they start to lose the attractiveness that drew people to them in the first place. The concept of **carrying capacity** can be used to examine this.

Not all people would agree on how large the numbers of visitors to a place would have to become before the attraction would start to become less attractive. This is known as the **perceptual carrying capacity** of a place. Thus bird watchers may believe that an area has a lower carrying capacity than a group of day-trippers. Perceptual carrying capacities can be raised by environmental improvements such as the planting of screening vegetation to make the visitor attraction *appear* less crowded than it actually

Resource 10: Perceptual carrying capacity exceeded? Marble Hill, Donegal 2001

is. The numbers of visitors that a place's environment can sustainably cope with is called the **environmental carrying capacity**. An environment can be changed to increase the environmental carrying capacity too. An example would be wooden walkways through dunes allowing more visitors to use the dunes with less damage to its ecosystem. A further version of carrying capacity is the **physical carrying capacity**. This refers to the numbers of visitors that the venue can serve. This may be dependent on factors such as the number of car parking spaces, the number of seats available in cafés and so on. Again this can be raised by the provision of more facilities thus allowing more visitors. However those who manage tourist venues have to be careful not to let a raised physical carrying capacity allow numbers to increase so much that perceptual or environmental carrying capacities are exceeded.

There are many ways in which tourism can cause environmental damage. Skiing is an increasingly popular winter tourist activity which, in Europe, is particularly developed in the Alps. The creation of ski slopes (pistes) and the infrastructure to carry skiers to the slopes (cable cars, car parks and so on) has meant the removal of large areas of trees. In summer this can create problems, as the trees are no longer present to reduce the likelihood of mudslides and flooding. In winter the avalanche risk is increased.

Pollution is another negative consequence of tourism. Planes transporting tourists to their destinations can cause significant noise pollution. Water pollution can be caused by the use of detergents by hotels. More tourists in an area mean more waste and more sewage. In some parts of the world, limited treatment of waste water means increased pollution.

However tourism can potentially improve the environment as money earned through tourism can be spent on improving the infrastructure, including the building of treatment plants and the conservation of ecosystems and the built environment.

Tourists use resources, which may be scarce, in the areas to which they travel. For example in Mallorca, one of the most popular package holiday destinations for tourists from northern Europe, pressure on water resources led to severe shortages in 1994. So much water had been extracted that local supplies were contaminated by salt and both local people and tourists had to rely on water imported from mainland Spain. The island has now built a desalination plant to overcome the difficulties and have also implemented water conservation measures. In one example, golf courses, which once consumed enormous amounts of local water to keep them green and attractive, now use only waste water.

Some tourism activities can threaten biodiversity. One small scale example is the proposed building of a funicular railway to allow easier access by tourists to the summit of Cairn Gorm, in the Scottish Highlands. Conservationists are concerned about the impact that additional visitors will have on the fragile mountain landscape and on birds such as the snow bunting, dotterel and ptarmigan. On a larger scale Florida's popularity as a tourist destination threatens the Everglades and its unique assemblage of plants and animals.

It might be thought that tourism offers the opportunity for different cultures to meet and to share but tourism can also have a negative impact on existing social structures. Tom Selwyn, an anthropologist who has researched the socio-cultural impact of tourism, has pointed out that "tourism can destroy communities very fast and whatever advantage is gained in the form of foreign exchange is often outweighed by the negative effects". Tourism can devalue local customs if they are performed for the amusement of visitors. It can also lead to an increase in petty crime and prostitution.

Increasing awareness of the potential negative effects of tourism has led to efforts to promote forms of tourism which use the environment sustainably. A number of forms of tourism that are alternatives to mass tourism have been developed. One of these is **ecotourism**, often related to natural landscapes such as nature reserves, game parks and so on. In some instances this form of tourism is closely related to conservation and has had some success in places like Belize. However ecotourism is largely restricted to wealthy individuals, and has been nicknamed egotourism. It has also been argued that the 'eco' part of ecotourism is often only a marketing ploy by tour companies. The destinations of ecotourism are often fragile and even small numbers of tourists can cause damage; paradoxically mass tourism, often seen as a more destructive force, concentrates people in a small area and so minimises the damage they cause to the wider environment.

Case study: Tourism in Nepal

The combination of cultural diversity and architectural and natural beauty has been bringing over 250,000 visitors to Nepal each year. Until 1950 most foreigners were excluded from Nepal; the first westerners were mountaineers scaling the Himalayan peaks. Since the 1960s a wider range of western visitors have visited Nepal. The typical Nepal tourist from the west is a young male backpacker but more and more Nepal is seen as a stopover point on long haul Asian or round-the-world tours. Trekking is one of the most popular activities for many tourists although rafting and mountain biking are also available. Despite Nepal's growing popularity as a destination by westerners and by Japanese tourists, 32% of tourists to Nepal come from neighbouring India.

Tourism is seasonal and, during the summer monsoon period, there are few trekkers because of the increased risk of flooding and of landslides. Visibility is also poor at this time of year and the leeches are particularly abundant.

Tourism is also regionally concentrated. Some parts of Nepal have few tourists as the limited road network restricts the movement of tourists into these areas. The most developed areas are around Kathmandu, the capital city, and Pokhara, close to the Annapurna Conservation Area – an important trekking centre.

Tourism can also be a fickle industry. For example the Maoist guerrillas, who have been fighting the Nepalese army since 1995 with the loss of 1700 lives, took advantage of the unrest following the shooting of members of the Nepalese Royal Family in June 2001 to stage an upsurge in violence. In consequence tourist figures that month fell to 10,238 compared to 23,715 in the June of the previous year.

Some aspects of tourism have been beneficial to Nepal.
- Employment has been provided. For example, mountain based tourism requires guides and porters and in many areas the indigenous people, Sherpas, have provided these. This has transformed some areas of Nepal from subsistence to cash economies;
- Previously high rates of outmigration have been curbed in those areas where tourism has been established;
- Local cultural monuments have been preserved.

In other ways however, tourism has had damaging effects
- With great differences in earnings between some of those involved in tourism and those engaged in agricultural activities, traditional social structures are under threat;
- Food prices have risen;
- Waste from trekkers and other tourists have diminished the quality of the environment: one trekking route has been nicknamed 'The Andrex trail';
- Water supplies have been contaminated by trekkers;
- The sustainability of wood supplies is threatened as rhododendron forests are consumed for fuel and tourist-related building. In one estimate a small village was said to consume one hectare of virgin rhododendron forest each year to service the needs of trekkers.

Resource 11: Nepal

The Nepalese government see tourism as an important element of their development strategy for the country. In the Five Year Development Plan from 1990 to 1995 the emphasis was on:

- encouraging high spending tourists (trekkers were found to spend only $20 per day in Nepal compared with twice that figure for those tourists who had not come on an activity holiday).
- strengthening the links between the hotels and local industry to encourage an employment multiplier effect in the country and to reduce leakage which was put, at one estimate, at 62%.

Since 1995, the Nepal Government has moved towards encouraging more private investment in tourism. Government input is now primarily restricted to the development of tourism infrastructure. While there had been earlier efforts to decentralise tourism, away from the Kathmandu valley for example, there is still considerable imbalance in tourist impact. Efforts to decentralise will continue in order to, as the Nepal Government's present Tourism Policy states, "diversify tourism down to rural areas so as to improve employment opportunities, foreign currency earnings, growth of regional income and [to reduce] regional imbalances". There is also a recognition that, if internal unrest continues, the long term prospects for tourism are bleak.

Chapter 4

Integrated Industry

All economic activities – primary, secondary and tertiary – have been subject to enormous change, especially over the last 50 years. Farming is being transformed into a highly industrialised operation, manufacturing has seen a shift away from traditional industries in MEDCs and tourism employs more people than any other economic activity. Many of the factors operating to produce these changes are linked to **globalisation** – the development of a single, worldwide economy.

Industry has long had an international dimension with companies trading goods and services across international boundaries. It is only comparatively recently that economic activities *within* a company have become dispersed between countries. Changes in transport and communication technology have made it possible for companies to locate different parts of their operations in a number of countries. These firms are called multinational, or sometimes transnational, corporations and it is their operations that form the basis of the **globalisation** of economic activity.

Multinational Corporations (MNCs) operate by having a parent firm, usually located in a MEDC, and affiliates in foreign countries. There are about 40,000 Multinational Corporations with 250,000 affiliates worldwide. Germany has the largest number of MNCs, at over 7000, followed by Japan, Sweden, Switzerland and the USA. Two thirds of world trade in goods and services is controlled by multinationals. One third of world trade is made up of transactions among different parts of the same corporations. Over 40% of trade is carried out by the biggest 350 companies.

Resource 12: Countries/Multinational Companies

Country or Corporation	Total GNP or total sales (US$ billion)
General Motors (USA)	161
DaimlerChrysler (USA)	155
Norway	152
Ford Motor Company (USA)	144
Saudi Arabia	143
Wal-Mart Stores (USA)	139
South Africa	137
Thailand	131
Royal Dutch Shell (Netherlands/UK)	128
Mitsui & Company (Japan)	109
Mitsubishi (Japan)	107
Exxon Mobil (USA)	101

Source: Fortune 500/1999/ UN Human Development Report 2000

The biggest multinational in 1999 was General Motors – an American MNC. It has a workforce of 372,000, many of whom were employed outside the USA in one of the over 30 countries in which it has manufacturing plants. In 1999 General Motors's assets of over US$183 billion were more than three times the GDP of New Zealand and five times that of Nigeria, a country of 110 million people. Indeed, of the 100 largest economies in the world, only 49 are countries. The rest are global corporations. **Resource 12** shows a selection of these.

These corporations are often more powerful than the countries in which they operate and this, and the international nature of their activities, can make their regulation by national governments difficult.

MNCs locate in foreign countries as a result of careful planning. They may
- have reached the plateau of local markets and be seeking new markets for their products;
- be setting up affiliate companies to escape protectionist measures in the foreign country. Taxes on imports protect indigenous firms but an affiliate company of a multinational will escape these taxes;
- be trying to reduce market competition by merging with or acquiring a foreign competitor;
- be reducing labour or other costs. MNCs can reduce the costs of their products and improve their market competitiveness by locating part of their activities abroad. It is for this reason that a lot of back office activities (**Resource 13**) and call centres are being set up in Ireland. These offices handle anything for clients in US cities, from insurance claims to complaints.

Resource 13: © Chris Duggan *The Daily Telegraph*

MNCs can have beneficial effects in the countries in which they operate. They bring employment and may introduce new technology. The skills that they bring, whether in management or in production, may spread to indigenous enterprises. There may be opportunities for growth in upstream (eg raw material production) or downstream (eg distribution) enterprises stimulating the local economy further.

However there are also potentially damaging effects of MNCs. Often the subsidiary factories opened by MNCs are exactly that – subsidiary to the main factory in the MNC's country of origin. If recession hits, the branch factory is the first to feel the effects of job cuts and closures, such as when Fruit of the Loom, a US clothes manufacturer, pulled out of the northeast of Ireland. Technology might not be made available to the subsidiary country as often the production stage in the subsidiary plant is labour intensive and the more profitable parts of the process are located in the home country. As Fruit of the Loom say on their website, one of their company's primary strengths is "low cost production resulting primarily from the offshore location of substantially all of its labor-intensive manufacturing operation".

Many MNCs locate in countries where environmental safeguards are not as rigorous as in their home areas. There is a concern that, in their efforts to attract MNCs, some countries are involved in a 'race to the bottom' as they relax, or fail to enforce, environmental protection measures. Some geographers also believe that grants and other incentives used to attract MNCs to locate in an area might be better utilised elsewhere in the economy. Linkages between local economies and MNCs are possible, but many of the more essential and lucrative suppliers may be acquired by the MNC as it follows a policy of horizontal and vertical integration.

Horizontal integration occurs when companies acquire or amalgamate with other firms that are involved in the same business as them. They may do this to increase market share, to benefit from economies of scale or to eliminate competition. For example we have seen how British Steel amalgamated with a Dutch steel company to form Corus – a much bigger player and more likely to survive in a difficult marketplace. Many companies around the world feel pressures to expand in this way and, such is the concern that competition will be stifled, many countries attempt to restrict the development of monopolies.

When manufacturing companies acquire or merge with other firms that supply them with materials (upstream) or that process, package, transport or market their materials (downstream) this is termed **vertical integration**. For example a manufacturer of breakfast cereals may find it more efficient to produce its own grain on farms that it controls (upstream) and to acquire firms to transport and market the finished product (downstream). An example of a vertically integrated enterprise is Gap. This US based clothing company uses 3,200 factories in 55 other countries to fabricate much of its clothing using cheap labour. The clothes are then sold in Gap stores – new outlets are opening at a rate of 120 to 150 each year – around the world.

Some people believe that globalisation has a negative impact on the environment and on the prospects for poor people in the world. While the lifting of restrictions on world trade by the World Trade Organisation (WTO) is seen as an opportunity by MNCs, others feel that moving to a more open system of trade will allow MNCs even freer movement

Resource 14: Cartoon by Paul Fitzgerald, *New Internationalist* August 2001

of their industrial activities around the globe. Protests outside the WTO meeting in Seattle, USA in November 1999 which was aiming to further liberalise world trade, targeted the premises of big companies (see cover photograph). Following violent protests at the G8 meeting in Genoa in 2001, there is speculation that the organisation of future inter-governmental meetings likely to be targeted in this way will have to be reconsidered.

There are fears that, with global corporations controlling most of the world's media, it will be increasingly difficult to challenge them.

Case study: Cargill

Cargill is a multinational manufacturer, processor and distributor. It employs 85,000 people in 59 countries and is involved with agricultural products including foodstuffs and animal feeds, and financial and industrial products. It is the largest oilseed processor in the world and the largest producer of malt – sprouted grain for the brewing industry. It is the producer and supplier of 10% of the world's supply of salt; the third largest flour milling operation in the USA; the owner of the largest cattle packing plant in Canada; the largest grain trader in the world and the largest pasta maker in Venezuela.

These superlatives disguise the fact that Cargill is not a household name unlike other MNCs such as Sony, Nestlé or Glaxo. Nevertheless it is a very important part of the world's global economy having earned $295 million in the first six months of the 2000 fiscal year, and it supplies, directly or indirectly, a significant proportion of our food. Started by WW Cargill in 1865 in Iowa, the firm first diversified, from operating grain warehouses, by building ships in La Crosse to transport the grain down the Mississippi. By 1890 Cargill was operating two flour mills. Further expansion led, in 1928, to the opening of its first affiliate – the Cargill Grain Company Ltd in Montreal, Canada. This was swiftly followed by other branches in Europe and South America.

In 1942 Cargill laid plans for six ocean-going tankers and constructed a shipyard on the Minnesota River, Port Cargill, to build them. As well as distribution, Cargill diversified into soya bean processing in one of a series of acquisitions and mergers. They became involved in the manufacture of feeds for livestock and poultry in the early 1950s. They introduced hybrid grain to Argentina in 1958 and formed another subsidiary, Cargill Agricola SA, in Brazil in 1965.

Just as feedstuff manufacture was a logical progression from grain production and distribution, further vertical integration led Cargill into the broiler chicken industry by a further acquisition in 1966. They then bought a Louisiana saltworks in 1971 to complement their food processing operation. A steelworks acquired in 1974 linked with the manufacture of ships to transport the grain, the processed feedstuffs and the livestock and poultry products.

Cargill purchased a cattle feedstuff processing business in 1974 and shortly afterwards acquired a beef processing industry. Coffee, cotton, rubber, wool, malted grain, petroleum, cocoa, pork, corn, canola seed and liquid sweeteners are all now part of the Cargill operation. They are involved with Taiwan, Argentina, Brazil, Canada, China, Kenya, Pakistan, Nigeria, Tanzania, Singapore, Malaysia, Peru, France, Germany and many other countries in trading and processing. They also own a number of mines, the outputs of which are processed into fertiliser.

Cargill Citrus Department had imported the first bulk shipment of frozen concentrated orange juice from Brazil to the USA in 1977. It now reportedly is one of the three companies that control almost all of Brazil's frozen concentrated orange juice exports and sends a tanker load of concentrate every five days from Santos, the port of Sao Paulo, to terminals in Europe and North America. Cargill is said to own four citrus farms in Brazil, the largest of which has over 1.3 million trees in 54 square kilometres of reclaimed ranch land tended by just 300 workers. It is alleged to be the 'largest single orange grove in the world'.

One of Cargill's most recent investments has been in research. In 1999 they presented The University of Minnesota with $10 million to expand their work on microbe and plant genes. The previous year they had entered into a joint venture with Monsanto, the agrochemical multinational, to create grain 'enhanced through biotechnology', and to process and market these. In the same year Cargill sold its global seeds business, excluding Canada and the USA, to Monsanto for US$1.4 billion. Brewster Kneen, the author of a book on Cargill, believes that this arrangement will allow Monsanto to concentrate on genetically engineered seeds while Cargill can concentrate on inputs such as fertiliser and can also trade and process the crops and convert these into meat which in turn is processed and marketed.

Some South American countries view the possibility of increased grain production as a significant opportunity and have welcomed MNCs such as Cargills. The planned development in El Pantanal, a vast tropical wetland in Brazil, Paraguay and Bolivia offers huge prospects for monocropping of grain. The area had not been developed for agriculture before because of the difficulties of transporting the grain to the markets in MEDCs. Cargill is promoting the Hidrovía project which aims to make navigable 3400 kilometres of the Paraguay and Paraná rivers, opening the area to development. Conservationists fear the reduction in biodiversity that will result from such a development. They cite the damage done to the Cerrados region of Brazil in the late 1970s when it became a major soya bean producer and 21.3 million hectares of ecologically rich land were lost.

As monoculture increases so too does consumption of agrochemicals such as fertiliser and pesticides. In Argentina, pesticide imports increased from just over $US50 million in 1985 to over US$200 million in 1995. The use of hybrid seeds also increases the inputs that farmers need. As the seed does not breed true, further supplies of seed have to be purchased each year. MNCs dominate the market for hybrid seeds.

Since Argentina approved Roundup Ready (RR) soya bean (Roundup is a weedkiller made by Monsanto) in March 1996, its adoption has been dramatic with 2 million hectares planted by 1998. Since RR soya bean does breed true, farmers in Argentina had to sign contracts acknowledging Monsanto's ownership of the GM technology, legally preventing them from saving the seed to sow the following year. Companies are seeking to install 'terminator technology' in their seeds which will mean that the seed will not germinate to provide another harvest. Cargill's investment in GM research will help to develop this biotechnology.

While progress by Cargill and others has been relatively straightforward in South America, they have not so readily become established in some other parts of the world. In India, for example, they have met with considerable opposition from farmers. It is reported that, in 1993, a Cargill operation to establish a port facility in Kandla Port in India was abandoned after pressure from the military, small scale producers and peasant farmers. There are reports of rallies of half a million farmers opposing Cargill's plans to replace their seed with genetically altered seed and other protests deterred Cargill from taking over salt production in Gujarat state. Environmentalist Vandana

Shiva has set up a group called Navdana, meaning 'Nine Seeds', which campaigns against genetic engineering and patent monopolies in agriculture. They have set up seed banks and moved to organic farming in thousands of villages in 'Freedom Zones' – areas which are free from chemicals, inputs from MNCs, hybrid seeds and, in the future, from genetically engineered and patented crops. Shiva has said: "... more than 3000 villages have declared that they will never obey laws that create monopolies on seed. They will never adopt genetically engineered seed". In November 2000, farmers' groups crossed India, Bangladesh and the Philippines in a 'People's Caravan for Land and Food without Poisons' which raised awareness of corporate control of the food chain and of GM crops. Some governments in South Asia seem to agree with the fears of the farmers. Sri Lanka banned the import of GM food in May 2001.

Cargill, of course, see things very differently. They believe that the new technologies and their extensive vertically integrated operations will help to feed the world in the future. The chairman of Cargill addressed the World Trade Organisation in 1999 speaking on 'Global Agriculture: Working towards a Sustainable Food System'. The vice chairman of Cargill said in 2000: "...we've intensified our work to build support for more open markets and global food trade. We fully believe that those efforts will improve the long-term outlook for Cargill and our farm and food customers."

Opponents of the globalisation of economic activity are concerned with the effect on local economies and on the environment. Many environmentalists remain unconvinced that genetically altered plants are safe and many farmers are concerned about a growing dependence on MNCs for seed supply. They argue that placing control of seed marketing in the hands of a few MNCs might have a profound impact on food security.

References and further reading

Agriculture
I Bowler, (1996) *Agricultural Change in Developed Countries*
Cambridge University Press
R Dalton, and C Canevet, (1999) Brittany: A case study in Rural Transformation
Geography 362.64
M Phlipponneau, (1975) Breton farmyard politics *The Geographical Magazine*
XLVII No 5
A Rae, (1999) Wetland Ecosystems *Geofile* 362
M Raw, and P Atkins, (1995) *Agriculture and Food* Collins Educational
Richardson and C Cavenet, (1970) *Scottish Geographical Magazine*
The problems of change in a Breton farming community Vol 86,

Manufacturing Industry
M Raw, (1993) *Manufacturing Industry: the impact of change* Collins Educational

Tourism
G Nagle, (1999) *Tourism, Leisure and Recreation* Nelson
A Stevenson, (1997) Annapurna Himalayan Journey *The Royal Geographical Magazine*
LXIX No. 6
C Tyler, (1989) Killing the goose … *Geographical Magazine* October

Integration of Industry
B Kneen, (1995) Captured by the Company *New Internationalist* Vol 267
B Kneen, (1998) *What is Monsanto up to now? Good question!* www.corpwatch.org
G Mohan, (2000) Dislocating Globalisation: Power, Politics and Global Change
Geography 85.2
New Internationalist Magazine (1997) *Globalisation – Peeling back the layers* Vol 296
Anon *Field of Dreams* www.grain.org